SIFTING SHADES

POETRY

By

Amanullah Khan

© 2013 Amanullah Khan
All Rights Reserved.

No part of this publication may be reproduced, stored in a retrieval system, or transmitted, in any form or by any means, electronic, mechanical, photocopying, recording, or otherwise, without the written permission of the author.

First published by Dog Ear Publishing
4010 W. 86th Street, Ste H
Indianapolis, IN 46268
www.dogearpublishing.net

ISBN: 978-1-4575-1945-1

This book is printed on acid-free paper.

Printed in the United States of America

To my daughters,
ROXANNA, SABRINA, AND AMANDA

My heartfelt appreciation to
Those who listened to my poems,
and made comments or suggestions.

And my deepest gratitude to my father, who started
teaching English to me when I was three

And my profound love to my mother, who sang
Punjabi poetry to me while I was still in her lap

CONTENTS

To the Critic ix

I

My Song is Your Song 2
Ravi River 3
Capturing Dreams 4
Mango 6
Moments of Solace..7
Mount Rainier I 8
Mount Rainier II 9
Harappa 10
Cycle 11
Epitaph 12
Safari 13
Fleeting Moments 14
Living 15

II

Infantile Wisdom 18
In Search of Soul 19
Humanity 20
Motif 21
Longevity 22
Vanity 23
Race to Nowhere 24
Then there was Themis 25
To the Element 26
Creator 27
Conversation with a Parrot 28
Contemplation 29

III

Jasmine 32
Butterfly 33
Bliss 34
Aspirations 35
Alluring Quilt 36
Dilemma 37
Floriography of a poem 38
Poem 39

IV

Autopsy	42
Burlap Igloo	43
Billy Goat	44
Paradox	45
Renewal	46
Tear Drop	47
One Plus One is Seldom Two	48
Strategist	49
Jury	50
Eternal Love	51
Infinity	53
Sin	54
Rule of Heart	55
Father's Chivalrous Acts	56

V

War of Worship	58
Torch	59
The Hand	60
Seeds of Freedom in a Barren Soil	61
Sapling of Love	62
Cancer	63
Compassion	64
Bridge Party	65

VI

Weeping Glacier	68
Grave Robbers	69
Hermits in the Open	70
Pain Killer	71
Hadiya Pendleton	72
Wish	73
Sufi Treasure	74
Lost Bliss	75
Pretensions	76
Sublime	77

TO THE CRITIC

Let me paint the roses;
Let me share my thorns
And my poem's canvas
My images will adorn.

Let the lines reflect
The rainbows of my dreams.
Let my pen scribe
My heart's chosen themes.

Let me frame the images
With accents of my rhyme.
Let me add the rhythm.
Let gifted ring the chime.

Let me add the pinks;
Let me add the blues.
Do not chain the pen;
Do not mute the hues.

Let me chase infinity.
Let the ideas soar.
Let me have the ecstasy.
Let my pen explore.

I

MY SONG IS YOUR SONG

Let me gather starry nights and days filled with glee.
Let me run once again in the pouring rain.
Let me chase flying seeds on the wings of plumes.
Let me gather northern lights of my effervescent years.

Let me find the lost prance in my tired feet.
Let me shower in confetti of my childhood giggles.
Let me remember butterflies of my fluttering heart.
Let me collect all the follies of my awkward age.

Oh! I miss all the treasures of my early days—
Eager dash to my house with the news of grades,
Priceless kiss from my mom, I can still remember,
And the tears of her joy embellishing my cheeks.

Borrow notes from your laughs, melody from your tears,
Sing it to your own tune and it will be your song.
Bring me the moments of my song and take all I have.
I will be the richest pauper. I will have it all.

RAVI RIVER

The edge of the water was set ablaze,
Lit by caressing of the evening sun,
Imparting the river a brilliant sheen.
The boat was riding on the golden beam.

The boat was moving—the river was still.

Creaking of the oarlocks having long ceased,
The oars were sleeping in the drifting boat.
Time looked on from the bank of the river,
Mesmerized by the beauty of the scene.

The boat was moving—the river was still.

The jasmine inhaled, harmonious breeze
Infusing the air with a scented breath.
The noise stayed away and the music played.
The logic was mute and the heart took stage.

The boat was moving—the river was still.

Moon had cast nimbus of serenity,
A dancing floor for the waltzing ripples.
Stars shimmered on the body of water,
Surfing the river to caress the boat.

The boat was moving—the river was still.

Hands on the clock have been circling fast.
Whenever I pause in the faster lane,
I peer through the fog at the book of time.
Flipping through the pages, I often see

The boat is moving—the river is still.

CAPTURING DREAMS

Eerie landscape, Jurassic view;
Heavy air, smoky hew;
Elephant leaves, twisted wood;
Trembling inside, scared I stood.

Rustling leaves, howling noises;
Sea of creatures, a thousand faces;
From a gadget in the air
Impetuous show, celestial affair.

Magic moves of a beam.
A shape resembling mine streamed.
Crowd swarmed the hologram,
Appendages examining the human form.

A creature with a kind demeanor
Advanced in a gentle manner,
Touching me with a forelimb,
Coaxing me to follow him

Everyone started pulling back.
I followed the leader in his track,
Swinging creatures from the trees,
Assuming they were greeting me.

Then there was a sudden glare;
Images formed in the air.
All of a sudden, the crowd cheered.
A retro of my life appeared,

Composed of mostly dreams of mine,
Unfulfilled and lost in time.
Show ended in thunderous applause.
I was lifted by a thousand paws,

Thrown and tossed in the air,
Bouncing, shouting in a scare.
Fell from bed to the floor,
Frightened like never before.

Thereafter I surmised
And I fully realized
Drifting above the troposphere
Were the dreams of yesteryear.

I simply wished I could find
Castles of my callow mind.
If I had the alien beam
To capture all my wandering dreams.

MANGO

I could hear the monsoon thunder
Announcing welcome relief.
In a distant summer,
I could see my barefoot youth
Running in a drenching rain
In the gardens of Kasur,

Searching under the majestic trees,
Mangos loosed from the branches
By the torrential rain
And the shaking gusts of wind.

Brief pauses of the rain
Followed by the mango feast.
Rolling mangos between hands
To soften their pulp.
Biting holes in their skins
To suck the delicious juice.

I have tried to sketch the images
But simply failed to paint
All the shades of the Mango
Making it the king of fruits.

MOMENTS of SOLACE

Dodging all the barbs of living
Avoiding apartheid stakes
Escaping the pesky web of relations

High from the Alps of enlightenment
On the wings of rare moments
Come swooping once again

As they come gliding in
All of those quarantined dreams
Embellish the valley of my solace

Mount Rainier

I

Loosed of the digital collar
And the wireless leash,
Strolled on a vibrant carpet
Laid by the fallen leaves.
Yellow, gold, shades of red
Sprayed on the sloping canvas.
Mixture of the fertile lava
And a plethora of decay
Furnished elements for the paint,
Summer having bid adieu,
Approaching winter nudged the sun
On a southerly course.
A shared kingdom of serenity,
Everyone was welcome.
Each whiff of mountain air
Cleansed my defiled lungs
Choked by the inhaled soot
In the urban labyrinth.

Mount Rainier

II

As I curled up the mountain,
Beholding glimpses of the vista,
Scenes made cameo appearances
On a roaming magical stage.
Plumes of smoke from the cottages,
Patches of the golden aspen,
And stunning waterfalls
Peered through the curtain of mist.
Music of the mountain streams
Whispered along the utopian path,
Rippled through my muddled mind,
Washing the clogging thoughts away.

HARAPPA

Civilization of Harappa
In the Indus Valley
Scattered pieces of the relics
Hinting past glory—
Drainage channels, raised wells
Suggesting sense of hygiene

"Welcome to the history museum,"
Proclaimed a distant voice.
Bewildered and confused, I asked,
"Who are you?"
"I am the future," he declared.
"It is a pity you cannot see," and he went on:,
"This was a thriving city
Built by the sweat of people
Hauling large stones.
Walls, moats, and the fort
To fend the invaders off,
Oblivious of the inner threats.

"What was coming, no one saw.,
History was repeating.
Civilizations rise and fall;
Now you see the aftermath.
Read the writing on the ruins.
Go and tell the living,
They can still break the cycle."

I was in a somber zone,
Contemplating the future.
Distant voice kept prodding,
"Do you hear, do you see?"
In a flash of realization, I bellowed out,
"I hear you! I do see!"

CYCLE

Handle turned away from world,
Bicycle leaning against the wall.
No one dares to stir the memories.
No one dares to touch.
Savage snap of link with the rider
Ended by the cycle of life.

Wheels frozen, tires deflated,
Worn in the dash to nowhere.
Dents on the aging frame
Evidenced knocks of life,
Flakes of decay falling off
From the languished metal.

Wrapping up the Orphic cycle
Of the array of atoms
Finishing their tour of duty,
Having fought infinite feuds.

Torn apart by the battles,
Atoms return—again—
Assuming their assigned position
In the periodic table,
Wait for another turn,
Hoping for a different outcome.

EPITAPH

Voyage on earth matters not
It is the footprint on the trail
Ask there be no tombstone
Let your deeds be the epitaph

SAFARI

Among the crumbling bones of mountain
There was a pile of animal chalk.
Was it a feared king of the jungle
Or a prancing playful calf?
Hard to tell from the heap.
Could have hauled a mighty elephant.
Now a part of amorphous stack,
It could be a wandering soul that
After travelling a million miles
Finally came to rest at home.
The only tale of his being
The trail strewn with his deeds.
Was it a mere killing machine
Or a loving charming doe?

FLEETING MOMENTS

Sun will fail to shine forever.
Fifteen minutes of fame shall wane.
Savor the glare, for in the dark,
Even the shadows part their ways.

LIVING

Savor the dewdrop on a rose.
Sip the rays of a rising sun.

Be like a child, enjoy the swings
Of all your rainbows of the dreams.

Write the lyrics, make the music.
Life can be full for a mere song.

II

INFANTILE WISDOM

At the sight of blinding lights
And alien faces,
You had wailed the first cry.

But others laughed it off!

Was it a reflexive action?
Or your innate wisdom,
Foretelling things to come?

IN SEARCH OF SOUL

Food fills anatomic pit;
Still it leaves an empty hole.
Eating imparts fleeting satiety
But you need to feed the soul.
Food sustains the body matter;
Love is needed to nourish the soul,

Ethereal, evasive, and unseen,
Yet it's there, held by all.
What is the enigma they call soul?
Remains a mystery, who will call?
Thought by some the cradle of emotion,
A castle of love, standing tall.

The issue of the soul have many pondered,
But the trail turned up cold.
Perceived only when it escapes;
Thus the story will never unfold.

Humanity

Break all the earthly shackles
Take the material mask off
Ride the clouds of ecstasy
Seek terrestrial heights

Be like the spring shower
Drench the world in bliss
Nurture gardens of the soul
And make love bloom

MOTIF

Passage through the trail of life
Strewn with the travail of life

Fortify, have the will of steel
Forge through the hail of life

Sway not; take a steadfast stand
In the mistral gale of life

Dare the wings of opposing wind
Unfurl tenuous sail of life

Imbue the soul with a meaning
Drink from the grail of life

Before ceding the trail of life
Leave a luring tale of life

LONGEVITY

A bushel of plums was on the table,
Soft skin tightly stretched,
Fresh and tangy, mouth-watering,
With a youthful glow.

A few were eaten every day.
Some were left behind.
Fewer and fewer were in the basket
Each passing day.

Although ripe and sweet with time,
Plums were losing sheen.
Notable was the loss in shape.
The silky skin was rough.

The last remaining was so wrinkled,
What a change with time.
Longevity is a cruel bargain.
Plum is bartered for a prune.

VANITY

Unfolding endowed helix
Implements inscribed code,
Defiance of the immutable force
Is the pursuit of a mirage.

Tightening leather cured by sun
Covering furrows carved by time,
Denying changes, hiding milestones,
Trying to mimic lost images.

Façade erected from the wreckage,
Supported by the decaying props;
Sheer deception or delusion,
A camouflage—a losing cause,

Succumbing to the lure of vanity,
Fooling the mirror on the wall.
The mirror simply spits back
The image of a made-up doll.

RACE TO NOWHERE

Circling at the fastest pace
Within the gerbil wheel of time,
All consumed in the footrace
Soul lurching far behind.

THEN THERE WAS THEMIS

A distant beacon from the Greeks,
Fingerprints of the Titaness Themis
Addressing clamor of the soul,
"A civilized order with equal justice."

Romans contributed Justitia,
Dispensing justice blindfolded,
Not beholden to a dogma or a particular view,
Serving each and every one knocking at the door.

Many constraints now hinder the steps
To the chambers of good counsel.
Imprints of the feudal tenure also linger on.
Plight of the downtrodden often goes unnoticed.

Should Justitia have some vision
To watch the dispossessed,
Allowing access to the chambers
Of the modern Themis?

TO THE ELEMENT

Mightiest mountain will crumble.
Tallest tree will also tumble.

One is destined to grow so tall.
The toll for growth is paid by all.

Blossom lest the spring be gone.
Fall in chase; the cycle is on.

Avail the moment, find your role.
Know not when the bell shall toll.

Elements have a fixed place.
Periodic table is the base.

Combination can be changed,
What you make, how it is arranged,

Whether a ploughshare or a sword,
Molten metal, how it is poured.

You can play a pivotal part,
To the element matters not.

CREATOR

When sunset paints horizon.
When spring adorns the valley.
When autumn sprays the forest.
When sky wears the rainbow.
When stars burst and sparkle
And moon gives the glow.
I wonder about the Creator,
Who puts up all the show.

I searched every dogma.
I looked high and low.
Many fervent arguments
But no one in the know.
I broke all the shackles
And let my soul grow.

I saw the eye's failings.
I saw inverted images.
I saw the missed clues.
I saw His gift to man.
I saw with inward eye.
It set my thoughts free.
Now I see His presence,
In every part of me.

CONVERSATION WITH A PARROT

Alluring sunset, bursting gold.
I was enamored with the scene.
A parrot in the nearby bush
Struck a conversation.

He had watched a shattering blast
High up from the sky.
"God's kingdom is being saved,"
He heard someone say.

Puzzled by the contradiction, he rightly asked,
"If God appoints the birthplace
And to whom you are born,
Doesn't that determine the flock to which you conform?

"I hear them say Almighty
Possessing all the power,
He can make it all happen.
Why does man impose?"

He made a sage statement.
The parrot was in the know.
Fluffed his feathers, raised his beak,
And he proclaimed,

"Thank you, Lord, for making me a parrot!"

CONTEMPLATION

When the time comes, as it should,
For God to be seen as all that's good,

Boats will turn from precipice's brink;
Man will sing and ocean will shrink.

Flotillas will reach the peaceful shore;
Dawn will be opening heaven's door.

Man will alight and kneel and pray,
Thank Almighty for the joyous day.

III

JASMINE

Velvety green with pearls in her lap,
Sensuous aroma travels afar,
Pulls one in and touches the heart.
Again and again, each year, each spring,
May she bloom, flourish, and spread,
Adorn each balcony, terrace, and bed.

In this prison of stench and stale
Suffocating passages, hard to inhale,
Grow, my Jasmine, grow unfettered.
Embrace each wall, column, and fence.
Spread your fragrance, oh I plea.
Let me breathe, set me free.

BUTTERFLY

Pupa, alter your form.
Open your wings, reveal your charm.
Flutter, fly flower to flower.
You are free; you have the power.
Paint the garden and show your art.
Spread your beauty and touch my heart.

Wondrous beauty that you see
Come next winter shall not be.
Shapes, colors, and all the other
Artful designs put together,
Arranged atoms impart the glow;
Fleeting union puts up the show.

Like all the petals, you shall fall,
Colorful wings, body and all.
Evanescent parts go their way;
Waiting water washes away
Down to the ocean—that's the rule—
Where it began, shall join the pool.

BLISS

First wink of gold at dawn
Causing sky to blush,
Opening fountain of vitality,
Offering life's nectar.

Colorful curtains being drawn
At the cusp of dusk,
Graceful slide into horizon
By the retiring sun.

Cheerleading, bouncing clouds
Twirling electric batons;
Moon flirting through the veil,
Playing hide-and-seek;

Waltzing stars in the sky;
A nightly jubilation
Inviting you to join the gala,
Celebrate life's gifts.

Ocean of bliss all around
Waiting for you to submerse.
Dissolve into sea of beauty;
Ride the waves of mirth.

ASPIRATIONS

Rugged yet. refined leaves
Adorn many landscapes,
Admired for the tropical look,
But the sweet and tangy fruit is
Trampled and ignored.
Lonesome Loquat often wonders:
Why was I brought
To an alien land,
Uprooted from my soil
And the nourishing moisture?

Fruit never touched the dirt
In my native land.
People picked the juicy fruit
As soon as it ripened.
Here, only a rare bird
Savors my sweetness.
But one day, my progeny,
By its richness and appeal,
Will be loved and cherished,
Earning a place at the table.

ALLURING QUILT

Global envy, high esteem
Founder's wisdom, pioneer's dream.,

Toil of statesmen at its peak.
Years to weave and years to tweak.

Each generation had a role,
Judicious stitch at the poll.

Why is the turmoil, why the brawl,
Look at the mirror on the wall.

DILEMMA

If the beauty is not why,
What is the reason for the eye?
If the eye cannot see,
Does the beauty cease to be?

FLORIOGRAPHY OF A POEM

Amaranth of a Victorian lover
Iris for a smitten heart
Acacia nestling dainty aura
Or the Aster whispering love.

Hues of feelings arranged in rows
And rainbows of the sentiments.
Some may be thorn-laden,
Others laid with petals.

Conceived in the scholarly towers
Or a prison's pen;
Some are picked, smelled, and tossed.
Others preserved in the book of time.

POEM

Fragrance of the finer sentiments,
Exuding from the floral words,
Carried by the waves of rhythm,
Synchronizing beats of heart.
Kissed by the longing lips,
Given eternal life.

Some are like the autumnal blaze,
Pleasing to the whim of time.
As the winter curtain drops,
Falling with the fading leaves,
Raked to the compost pile.
Leaving bare stumps.

IV

AUTOPSY

Fatal stab and a bullet hole,
Both had sought a dominant role.

Both of them lay on a cold slab,
No more argument, no more jabs.

All the arguments were so flawed,
A nick of knife tore the façade.

The pigment varied, but so slight
Different shades of dark and light

Ribbed cages were laid open,
Similar scheme of cognate organs.

Mangled by the bestial action,
Looted of their vital function.

How can pigment cause such pain,
Minute amount miscue the brain?

BURLAP IGLOO

Frigid air
Shroud of snow covering the urban scene
Silence except feet crushing
Hidden layer of ice

Icicle-draped burlap bag
Was lying in a forgotten alley
Muffled chatter of the teeth from the motionless ball
Failing to reach the fur-covered ears of the passerby

Languid motion stretched the burlap
Shedding crystals of ice
Rose to assume a human form
Exposing purple feet

Begging for the elusive warmth
Trudged toward a store front
Frosted, cracked, chafed hand
Reached for a shoe display

Thudding against the prohibiting glass
Exacerbating pain

BILLY GOAT

Homage to a Sufi poet
At his final resting place
I walked among the ancient graves
Crumbling in the blistering sun.

Goats grazing withered grass
Among the humps of rolled soil.
One of them with a grown beard
Appeared to be the alpha goat.

There stood the imperious buck
Fore-hooves on a marble grave
Reaching for the tree branches
Forging on the greener leaves.

The grave of a proud chief
Who rode a two-humped camel.
A billy goat was now mounted
On his marble hump.

PARADOX

Prancing in the vast savanna of Serengeti,
Attached to his nursing mother by the invisible cord.
Budding life in the jungle, enjoying nature's plenty,
Oblivious of the lurking danger in the brown bushes.

Hungry cubs were in the den, lioness on the prowl.
She lunged at the fledgling morsel with lightning speed,
Powerful jaws snapped shut, choking off the air,
Unclasped the deadly bite when the deer ceased to move.

Back toward the fleeing herd, horror on her face,
Dazed eyes of the mother watched the gruesome end.
Maternal instinct ready to attack, survival froze her hooves.
The gory scene was being shown on a TV channel.

Everyone in the room gasped disapproval.
Someone turned the TV off, resigning in the sofa,
While savoring fine aroma coming from the kitchen,
Leg of venison from the hunt roasting in the oven.

RENEWAL

Cherish each valley, hill, and pond.
Explore the universe and beyond.
Waterfalls, rivers, rapids, and trails—
Enjoy the beauty, lest you bewail.

Etched indelibly on the slate,
Every creature carries his fate.
To enforce the plan, it shall call
Sooner or later, each and all.

Yields to none, no force or might.
Doomed are those who dare to fight.
Fret not content of the scroll.
Unknown is what makes it whole.

Elements that are trapped in you
Shall be part of the grass or dew,
Maybe from the magnolia tree
Gush as a fragrance to be free.

TEAR DROP

Teach me, O tear
Reach my soul,
Secret of the sparkle
Happy or morose.

ONE PLUS ONE IS SELDOM TWO

That motion is still, a perpetual illusion.
Everything still is in orbit
Or has an orbit within.
Thus the life keeps rolling on.
Elements exist; nothing is new.
What appears new is the sum of some.

One plus one is neither one, biologically.
Fused, consumed, and a new offspring
Stirred genes of disparate two,
Make a new chimerical one.
In the end, it's the only game—
The game of the only one.

STRATEGIST

Pierce the barrier, seize the thought.
Poll every voting phase.
Clear strategy we shall have
To guide you through the political haze.

Cram the policy that we feed.
Ruminate lines as they read.
Snow the audience, freeze the brains.
Come next election, they'll heed.

High-ground seekers will be stranded.
Amateur will not stand the heat.
When the exit polls anoint,
You will have the coveted seat.

JURY

Jumbled theories, figures and facts
Barrage of experts serve the buyers

Lofty ambitions, love of green
Compost heap of drive and greed

Theatrical acts, lexical salvos
Hard at work to fog your thought

Follow the instructions thrust by code
And you filter right from wrong

Guilt or innocence—decision is yours
Untangle web of truth and lore

If you ask, you shall receive
Answers through the legal sieve

ETERNAL LOVE

Wires
Tubes
Pumps and bellows
Sustained thread of waning life.

Her flaccid arms
Did not rise to give a comforting hug.
Her eyes did not tear up with the flood of affection.
Disengaged empty sockets, I could not bear to look.

Leaded apron of grief weighing on my chest,
I bowed down to touch Mother's feet,
And I saw her toes move.
Was it an acknowledgment of her favorite son?

Held her feet in my hands for my own solace.
Feet I believe will escort me to the gates of heaven.
Feet as a genetic trait she had gifted me.
Feet that will always guide me till we meet again.

My father gave me a near smile, but his eyes betrayed,
Could not peel his fixed gaze from my mother's face,
Guarding with his withered eyes
Nucleus of his being.

His eyes poured lava of grief
As he held the wilted hand like a delicate flower.
He at times pressed his face against the helpless hand.
Steady string of pearls of love pouring from his eyes.
I kept whispering lies of love.
She'll be OK! She'll be OK!

A few months later,
The phone rang;
"Daddy had a heart attack
He is also gone."

His heart was strong and healthy,
But loving heart was shattered.
Half of it was left behind,
Trapped in a bony cage.

Grace of love had prevailed,
Shown its glorious magic,
Gathered pieces of the heart
And made it whole again.

Should I mourn my greatest loss?
Or rejoice the eternal union of a broken heart?
I find the answer in a photo hanging on my wall,
Triumph of eternal love glowing on their faces.

INFINITY

Cove of solitude
Blissful moment
Breath embracing breath
Interweaving souls
Epitome of a lover's heart
A petal in the book of time
Preserving fragrance in its pages
Defining notion of infinity

SIN

Hint of sadness on the face
Tells of bottled pain;
Faded iris drained blue
A smile without the dimples.

Vain effort at disguise
Anguish pierces veil.
Gloomy score on the face
Discerning eye can read.

Every sin deserves forgiveness
But the greatest sin of all—
The sin of breaking vase of love,
The most fragile vessel.

Cradle love in a million petals
Speak in the gentlest tones.
Love's abode is a brittle castle
Careless words can shatter.

RULE OF HEART

Heart's yearning unexpressed
Pristine bouquets left to dry
Both wisdom and timidity
Are the nemeses of the heart

Laying yearning on the altar
Is irreverent and prohibited
Sovereign heart makes the rules
In the dominion of the love

FATHER'S CHIVALROUS ACTS

Cold, cold bath at the village well,
Before the dawn and the rooster's crow:
Father's chivalrous acts I tell.

Rusting bicycle, he rode as well.
Before the daybreak, miles to go;
Cold, cold bath at the village well.

He rode with the speed of gazelle.
Freezing weather in winters though,
Father's chivalrous acts I tell.

Family's love on his lapel,
With warmth of love, his face aglow;
Cold, cold bath at the village well.

Worn from the ride, his knees would swell.
Years were telling him to be slow;
Father's chivalrous acts I tell.

To be a father before I spell,
Many more miles I have to go;
Cold, cold bath at the village well;
Father's chivalrous acts I tell.

V

WAR OF WORSHIP

A mosque on the north, a church on the south,
And a tranquil path lay between the two.
Convocation of souls with muted mouth.
In praising the Creator, the faith grew.
Belief was nestled at a chosen place
Not on forehead but the altar of heart.
Everyone had the freedom to embrace
The direction they chose; it mattered not.
Cobblestone street bearing the same worn path
Social network that once was is no more.
Merchants of religion spewing the wrath
Eroded the worship down to the core.
Entrenched forces with a similar goal;
Pursuit of heaven, but a hellish toll.

TORCH

Blazing atmosphere
Astringent rhetoric
Seething crossfire
Seared tranquility
Desert of despair
Singed aspirations
Charred dreams
Spanning the globe
Signs of time
Find me an oasis
Find me shade

THE HAND

Cloud of horror dissipating
Smell of ash was still prevailing

Blast of a bomb had caused the scare
Blowing the remains in the air

Fire breathing monster, hatred's sake,
Killing the blameless in its wake

A severed limb was lying still
Mangled up like a roadside kill

Ring finger singed, the flesh was torn
The gathered crowd was full of scorn

Ring was studded with precious stones
Still clinging to the bare bone

Single stem of a fallen rose
Not in the hand, and yet so close

Missing petals, only the thorns
Instead of love a site to mourn

Faded henna, the palm still bore,
The dreams that were but were no more

The hand was looking to the sky,
Mournfully begging. Tell me why?

SEEDS OF FREEDOM IN A BARREN SOIL

Tongues are tied but allowed to breathe
To live in silence, soul will seethe
Dragon's rule, humanity's bane
Freedom lies shackled in a chain

Phantom borders drawn in the sand
Unseen barbs encircle the land
Ruse of a dragnet in the air
Peaceful doves are caught unaware

Olives of the soil have blood stains
The land of prophets, evil reigns
Man is making a salmon's leap
Spawning freedom, future will reap

Lambs are taking valiant stand
Painful wait for a helping hand

SAPLING OF LOVE

Gift from his nascent love
When he turned twenty
A treat for his eager eyes
Planted in the yard

He kept counting emerging leaves
All through the summer
Waiting for the next spring
To savor its blooms

All dreams torn asunder
On that fateful day
He ascended to the heavens
In the tower's plumes

Now he watches from above
The flower-laden bush
His mother minds all alone
Remnant of his dreams

Every morning tends flowers
Wiping tears of dew

CANCER

Preying on the unsuspecting
Exploiting genetic vagaries
Camouflaged insidious foe
Roosting in the helix
Perfidious mutant of the self
Pillages parent's nest

Laying primordial daughter cells
Spreading evil seed
Evading achromatic soldiers
Crosses sanguineous moats
Despised mother of all thieves
Steals innocent smiles

Trusting lives to my care
Daunting expectations
See the fugitive in their eyes
And I surmise
Can't pretend to be them
Yet they become part of me

COMPASSION

I see the phantom, hear the pain—
Woeful expressions, sunken eyes.
Hard to turn away from the anguish,
Be oblivious to the cries.

The Healthcare is on life support,
Yet blood is sucked to fuel the greed;
Hubris gutting the inner core,
Curbing access to those who need.

Nestled along the sloping hills
With a prime view of pristine shore
In the valley of pretension,
Insatiable want is the score.

Fenced lawns and the blood-money moats,
Opulent castles out of sight,
Armed guards are hindering access
Far removed from the human plight.

BRIDGE PARTY

Gliding with clouds, a fancy dream;
I had two wings, how real it seemed.

Surging below me, I could see
Vast river of humanity,

Full of color, beaming with life,
Carnivals, parades, without strife.

Some from the banks of the river
Shouted slogans with a fervor,

From right to left and left to right,
Shooting arrows with all their might.

Arrows were flying to and fro,
Some falling on people below,

Breaching harmony and the flow.
Could not tell a friend from the foe.

Saw the fracas, to my dismay;
High in the clouds I could not stay,

Wondering, Can one make them see?!
Stunning mosaic, we can be.

It was apparent, the two discrete
Banks of the river shall not meet.

Need was obvious, leave the bank,
Listen to the opposite flank.

I could see a bridge was needed
For the voices to be heeded.

Willed my body to be a part
Of a bridge of the gentle hearts;

Pleaded sanity, end of rift,
And the people honored the shift.

Both right and left approached the bridge,
Renouncing the dogmatic ridge.

Feat of reason to my delight;
No more arrows, no more fight.

VI

WEEPING GLACIER

Dregs of luxury in the air
Grating glacier's eye.
Doleful river of the tears
Flowing down its face.

Pristine stream from the mountain
Bouncing down the rocks
Will it vanish with the ice cap?
Will it be a tale of woes?

GRAVE ROBBERS

Reap the land and the sea,
But the womb, let it be.
Why to drill piercing bore?
Suck the sap from the core.
Feral want does not care,
Rattling earth's deeper layer.
Could it cause change in shape,
Let the scalding lava escape,
Moving plates causing shakes,
What they call an earthquake?
Once alive, eons old,
Buried tales never told—
Black gold is what they crave
While they rob the lineal grave.

HERMITS IN THE OPEN

Hydraulics and pistons multiply.
Human muscles atrophy.
Through the telescope of evolution
You can see the wasted limbs!

Buildings rising like ant hills,
Such a dizzying pace.
Wheels turning fast and furious
Up and down the terrain.

Burning fossil, suffocating
Visible air to breathe
Environmental sewers, above the tarmac
Rising higher and higher.

Menacing soot, defacing sun.
Vital rays are under siege
Confused are the sunflowers,
Facing every which way.

PAIN KILLER

Older than the man's footprints,
Meandering through the plains,
Carrying loads of Himalayan silt,
Enriching soil of the Punjab.

Flowing from the hills to sea,
Quenching thirst of land and life.
Bent, broken, and encroached,
Polluted by industrial filth.

Beauteous banks have been mauled
By the urban sprawl.
Turbines of the human want
Have been churning nature's will.

Symbiosis is the rule
For all life under the sun,
But for the menace of man
Disrupting nature's harmony.

Willow wept at man's agony,
Gave its skin to relieve the pain—
Eternal gift to a selfish species—
Lying parched at the banks, unable to cry.

HADIYA PENDLETON

Nightmare!
    Mirage of opulence
    Beehives reaching sky
    Suck the nector of dawn
    Denying Southside crypts
    Roots decaying
    Pent-up energy in the fruit - rotting

    Hiding her petite body
    From the flying lead
    Another bud fell to dust
    Another star crashed
    Into the heavy atmosphere
    Incinerating hope
Wake me up!

    Dawn rising from the Southside
    Sprinkling golden rays
    Reaching into forbidden lanes
    Hope sprouting
    Ambition blossoming
    Abundance of nectar
    Beehives offering honey
    Sparkles on the faces
See my dream!

WISH

Let us have a day of peace
Send the soldiers on a furlough
Or have them build a bridge
Let the preachers address the flock
But read a halcyon verse
Mute the megaphone of the politics
Let the caustic discourse cease
Let us have a day of peace

SUFI TREASURE

Diamond seeker dug the mountain
In the search for paltry stone.
The jewel of soul remained buried
Under the mound of phony self.

Tear the façade of the vanity.
Erase traces of the ego.
Achieve the status of sublime.
Frolic with the twirling souls.

LOST BLISS

When you are laid in absolute solitude
Covered with the mound of love
In the web of some relations,
Fibrils of the frayed emotions
May linger above the soil.
But the hammer of the time
Will close the last chapter
And nail the final lid.

Nightly luminaries in the sky
Will impart their glow.
Morning breeze caressing flowers,
Wafting fragrance on its wings,
Will keep rustling leaves and make soft music.
And birds will sing their morning songs.
Did you ever take a pause and savor beauty
While still above the surface of the covering sod?

PRETENSIONS

Thoughtless combat, gloating the loot,
Breaking the back to hoard in vain,
Expanding stockpile of the globules
In a surplus flapping rump.

Stomping on earth with fanciful pride,
Pretending to be the master
While the ravenous soil microbes
Wait for the ultimate feast.

But for the extensions of the self
Bewailing the snared silken thread,
There will be some mournful pretentions
Among the parade of spying visitors.

Marching by with long faces,
Bidding you farewell,
Dying to go back to chores,
Deaf to the tick of the clock.

SUBLIME

If and when I am permitted
To make the blissful moment stay,
Abandoned soul is levitated
To a hovel of straw and clay .

In a luscious peaceful valley
Cradling ambrosial dreams,
I hear the songs of serenity
Of the mountain streams.

I sit across a natural bridge,
Rustic bridge of a fallen tree.
I tear all the material bondage,
Setting the rusting soul free.

CPSIA information can be obtained at www.ICGtesting.com
Printed in the USA
LVOW08s2250101213

364799LV00001B/238/P